Pebble® Bilingüe/Bilingual Plus

Dientes sanos/Healthy Teeth

Antojitos para dientes sanos / Snacks for Healthy Teeth

por/by Mari Schuh

Traducción/Translation:
Dr. Martín Luis Guzmán Ferrer

Editor Consultor/Consulting Editor:
Dra. Gail Saunders-Smith

Consultor/Consultant:
Lori Gagliardi CDA, RDA, RDH, EdD

CAPSTONE PRESS
a capstone imprint

Pebble Plus is published by Capstone Press,
151 Good Counsel Drive, P.O. Box 669, Mankato, Minnesota 56002.
www.capstonepress.com

092009
005618CGS10

 Books published by Capstone Press are manufactured with paper
containing at least 10 percent post-consumer waste.

Library of Congress Cataloging-in-Publication Data
Schuh, Mari C., 1975–
    [Snacks for healthy teeth. Spanish & English]
    Antojitos para dientes sanos = Snacks for healthy teeth / por Mari Schuh.
    p. cm. — (Pebble Plus bilingüe. Dientes sanos = Pebble Plus bilingual. Healthy teeth)
    Summary: "Simple text, photographs, and diagrams present information about healthy snacks for teeth
and includes how to take care of teeth properly — in both English and Spanish" — Provided by publisher.
    Includes index.
    ISBN 978-1-4296-4599-7 (lib. bdg.)
    1. Nutrition and dental health — Juvenile literature. I. Title. II. Title: Snacks for healthy teeth. III. Series.
RK281.S2918 2010
617.6'01 — dc22   2009040924

Editorial Credits
Sarah L. Schuette, editor; Katy Kudela, bilingual editor; Adalin Torres-Zayas, Spanish copy editor;
    Veronica Bianchini, designer and illustrator; Eric Manske and Danielle Ceminsky, production specialists

Photo Credits
Capstone Press/Karon Dubke, all

The author dedicates this book to her husband, Joseph Quam.

Note to Parents and Teachers

The Dientes sanos/Healthy Teeth set supports national science standards related to
personal health. This book describes and illustrates healthy snacks for dental health in
both English and Spanish. The images support early readers in understanding the text.
The repetition of words and phrases helps early readers learn new words. This book also
introduces early readers to subject-specific vocabulary words, which are defined in the
Glossary section. Early readers may need assistance to read some words and to use the
Table of Contents, Glossary, Internet Sites, and Index sections of the book.

Table of Contents

Tabla de contenidos

Good Snacks

Teresa eats good snacks. They keep her teeth and gums healthy and strong.

Buenas meriendas

Teresa merienda alimentos sanos. Éstos conservan sus encías y dientes sanos y fuertes.

Teresa eats vegetables that are full of vitamins. Vitamins help her body fight diseases, even in her mouth.

Teresa come verduras que están llenas de vitaminas. Las vitaminas le ayudan al cuerpo a combatir las enfermedades, hasta en la boca.

Teresa's mouth makes more saliva when she eats fresh fruit. Saliva washes away sugar that causes decay.

La boca de Teresa produce más saliva cuando come frutas frescas. La saliva se lleva el azúcar que causa caries.

Teresa likes milk, cheese, and yogurt. These foods have calcium. Calcium makes teeth strong.

A Teresa le gusta la leche, el queso y el yogurt. Estos alimentos tienen calcio. El calcio fortalece los dientes.

Teresa snacks on popcorn.

It doesn't stick to her teeth

like gooey sweets.

Teresa merienda palomitas.

No se le pegan a las encías

como los dulces pegajosos.

Sweets

Sweets like candy and soda
can hurt the enamel
that protects your teeth.

Los dulces

Los dulces, como los caramelos o
los refrescos, pueden hacerle daño
al esmalte que protege tus dientes.

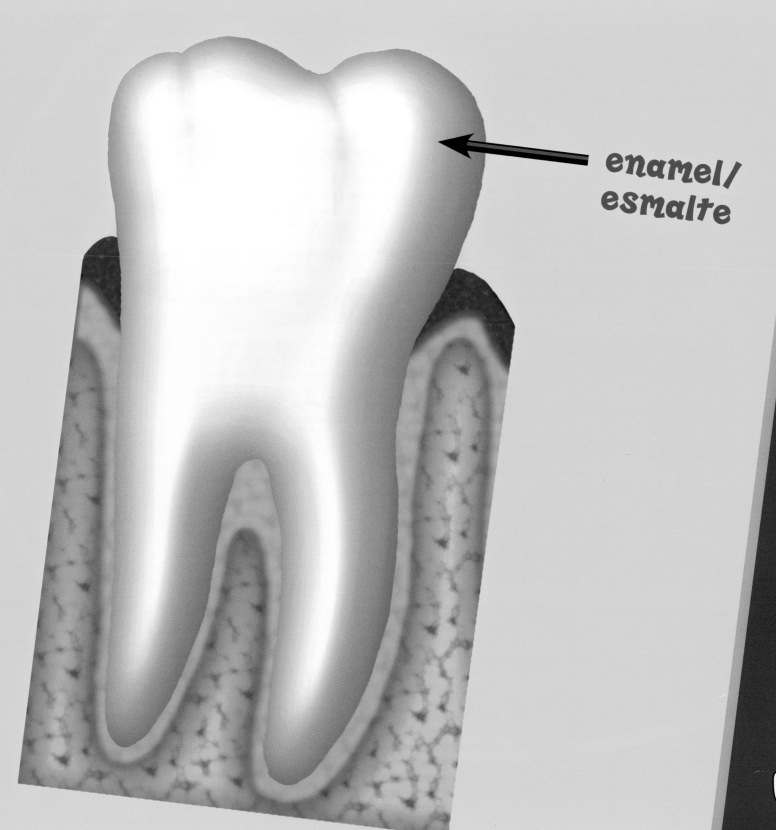

enamel/
esmalte

15

Germs in your mouth turn sugar
into acid. Acid wears away enamel.
Acid causes decay and cavities.

Los gérmenes que hay en tu boca
convierten el azúcar en ácido. El ácido
desgasta el esmalte. El ácido provoca
deterioro y caries.

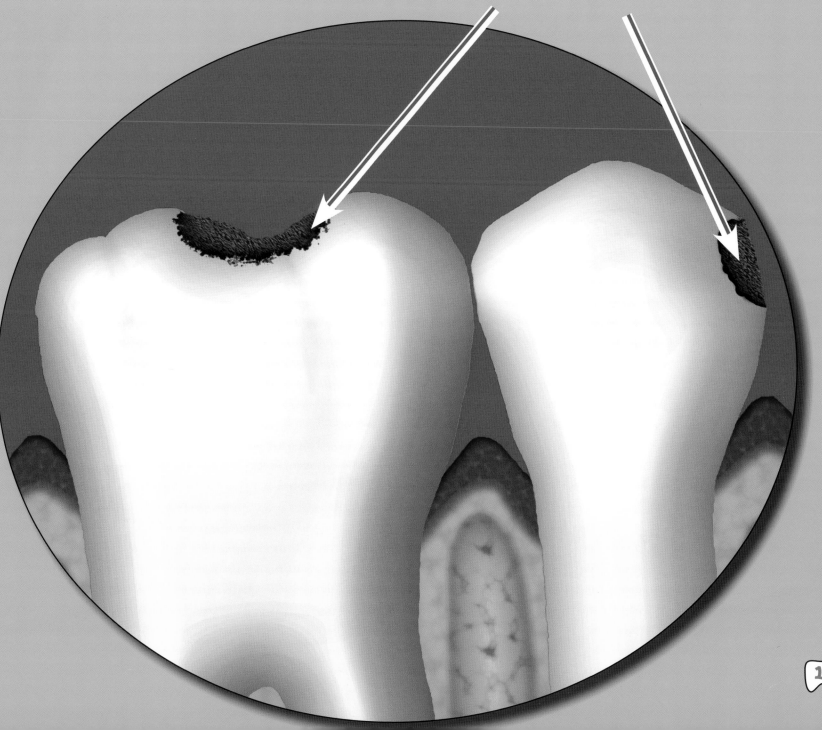

cavities/caries

17

Healthy Teeth

Teresa brushes her teeth to get rid of the acid. Even rinsing with water helps.

Dientes sanos

Teresa se cepilla los dientes para quitarse el ácido. Hasta enjuagárselos con agua ayuda.

Follow Teresa's good example and eat good snacks. You'll have strong, healthy teeth your whole life.

Sigue el buen ejemplo de Teresa y merienda bien. Así tendrás dientes fuertes y sanos toda tu vida.

Glossary

acid — a liquid that wears away teeth; acid forms from germs and sugar in your mouth.

cavity — a decayed or broken-down part of a tooth; eating healthy snacks helps prevent cavities.

decay — to rot, break down, or make a hole in something

enamel — the hard, glossy covering on teeth; enamel protects teeth from decay.

gum — the firm skin around the base of teeth

saliva — the clear liquid in your mouth that keeps it moist, helps you swallow, and digest food

sweets — foods that have lots of sugar

vitamin — a part of food that keeps you strong and helps protect you from getting sick

Internet Sites

FactHound offers a safe, fun way to find Internet sites related to this book. All of the sites on FactHound have been researched by our staff.

Here's all you do:

Visit *www.facthound.com*

FactHound will fetch the best sites for you!

Glosario

el ácido — líquido que desgasta los dientes; el ácido se forma con los gérmenes y el azúcar que hay en tu boca.

la carie — parte carcomida o agujero en el diente

el deterioro — pudrirse, romperse o hacer un hoyo en algo

los dulces — alimentos que contienen mucha azúcar

la encía — piel firme que rodea la base del diente

el esmalte — la cubierta dura y brillosa que cubre al diente; el esmalte protege a los dientes de deterioro.

la saliva — líquido claro de tu boca que la mantiene húmeda, y te ayuda a tragar y digerir la comida

la vitamina — parte de los alimentos que te mantiene fuerte y ayuda a protegerte de las enfermedades

Sitios de Internet

FactHound brinda una forma segura y divertida de encontrar sitios de Internet relacionados con este libro. Todos los sitios en FactHound han sido investigados por nuestro personal.

Esto es todo lo que tú necesitas hacer:

Visita *www.facthound.com*

¡FactHound buscará los mejores sitios para ti!

Index

acid, 16, 18
brushing, 18
calcium, 10
cavities, 16
cheese, 10
decay, 8, 16
diseases, 6

enamel, 14, 16
fruit, 8
germs, 16
gums, 4
milk, 10
popcorn, 12
rinsing, 18

saliva, 8
sugar, 8, 16
sweets, 12, 14
vegetables, 6
vitamins, 6
yogurt, 10

índice

ácido, 16, 18
azúcar, 8, 16
calcio, 10
caries, 16
cepillarse, 18
deterioro, 8, 16
dulces, 12, 14

encías, 4
enfermedades, 6
enjuagarse, 18
esmalte, 14, 16
frutas, 8
gérmenes, 16
leche, 10

palomitas, 12
queso, 10
saliva, 8
verduras, 6
vitaminas, 6
yogurt, 10